Hello, Family Members,

Learning to read is one of the most important accomplishments of early childhood. **Hello Reader!** books are designed to help children become skilled readers who like to read. Beginning readers learn to read by remembering frequently used words like "the," "is," and "and"; by using phonics skills to decode new words; and by interpreting picture and text clues. These books provide both the stories children enjoy and the structure they need to read fluently and independently. Here are suggestions for helping your child *before, during,* and *after* reading:

Before

- Look at the cover and pictures and have your child predict what the story is about.
- Read the story to your child.
- Encourage your child to chime in with familiar words and phrases.
- Echo read with your child by reading a line first and having your child read it after you do.

During

- Have your child think about a word he or she does not recognize right away. Provide hints such as "Let's see if we know the sounds" and "Have we read other words like this one?"
- Encourage your child to use phonics skills to sound out new words.
- Provide the word for your child when more assistance is needed so that he or she does not struggle and the experience of reading with you is a positive one.
- Encourage your child to have fun by reading with a lot of expression . . . like an actor!

After

- Have your child keep lists of interesting and favorite words.
- Encourage your child to read the books over and over again. Have him or her read to brothers, sisters, grandparents, and even teddy bears. Repeated readings develop confidence in young readers.
- Talk about the stories. Ask and answer questions. Share ideas about the funniest and most interesting characters and events in the stories.

I do hope that you and your child enjoy this book.

—Francie Alexander
Reading Specialist,
Scholastic's Instructional Publishing Group

If you have questions or comments about how children learn to read, please contact Francie Alexander at FrancieAl@aol.com

To Joanna
— D. W.

For Megan
— J.R.

Photo credits:
Page 41: © Steven Caras/Courtesy of The New York City Ballet
Pages 42, 48, and cover: © Paul Kolnik/Courtesy of The New York City Ballet

Text copyright © 1998 by Diana White.
Illustrations copyright © 1998 by Jacqueline Rogers.
All rights reserved. Published by Scholastic Inc.
HELLO READER! and CARTWHEEL BOOKS and associated logos
are trademarks and/or registered trademarks of Scholastic Inc.

Library of Congress Cataloging-in-Publication Data

White, Diana.
    Ballerina dreams / by Diana White; illustrated by Jacqueline Rogers.
        p.   cm.— (Hello reader! Level 3)
    Summary: Diana White recounts how her dream of becoming a
ballerina came true, from her first dance class at age four to her work
with the New York City Ballet.
    ISBN 0-590-37233-5
    1. White, Diana—Juvenile literature.   2. Ballerinas—United States—
Biography—Juvenile literature. [1. White, Diana. 2. Ballet dancers. 3.
Ballet dancing.] I. Rogers, Jacqueline, ill. II. Title. III. Series.
GV1785.W44A3   1998
792.8'092—dc21
[B]   97-24002
                                                                            CIP
                                                                             AC

10 9 8 7 6 5 4 3 2   8 9/9 0/0 01 02

Printed in the U.S.A.   24
First printing, September 1998

Ballerina Dreams

by Diana White

Illustrated by Jacqueline Rogers

Hello Reader!—Level 3

SCHOLASTIC INC.

New York Toronto London Auckland Sydney

My name is Diana White.

I am a ballerina with the New York City Ballet.

As a little girl, my dream was to
become a ballet dancer.

This is the story of how my dream came true.

I grew up in Park Ridge, Illinois.
My mom says that I started
dancing as soon as I could walk.
One day I fell and hit my head on a table.
My parents rushed me to the hospital.
My face was badly bruised
and I had to wear a big bandage.

At the time, the doctors did not
know that I had hurt my eyes, too.
But soon, people began to tell my
mother that I looked cross-eyed.
The accident had hurt my eyesight
and I could not see well.
I had to wear *very* thick glasses.

I saw my first real ballet
when I was three years old.
Wearing my best dress,
I took the train with my mother.
The ballet was in the Auditorium Theater
in downtown Chicago.
The seats in the front rows were too expensive.
We sat in the balcony at the back of the theater.
I didn't mind.
I was so happy to be there!

The ballet was called *Sleeping Beauty*.
All of the dancers wore tutus of
blue, yellow, or white.
I loved hearing the music and
seeing the beautiful costumes.
Then I saw the one ballerina in the bright spotlight.
At that moment, I knew.
More than anything, I wanted to be that ballerina.

One year later, I started taking
ballet lessons once a week.
On the first day, I wore a big, blue tutu.
The class was in a large room.
A mirror covered one whole wall.
A long, wooden pole called a
barre ran along another wall.

Before class began, we moved
around to warm up our bodies.
This was so we didn't hurt our
muscles when we danced.
To warm up our feet, we raised
our heels off the floor.
My teacher, Miss Willow, said
"boogie" when our heels went up.
Then she said "woogie" when our
heels came down.
We also learned a step called *balancé*.
For this step, we swayed our bodies
back and forth.
Miss Willow even made up a song:

> *Balancé. Balancé.*
> *Swaying so gracefully.*
> *Balancé. Balancé.*
> *Just like a willow tree.*

I thought that was funny because
my teacher's name was Miss Willow.
She was very graceful.

I asked my dad to put a *barre* on my bedroom wall
Now I could practice on my own.
I danced all the time —
even walking down the stairs in my house!
Whenever I had to go downstairs,
I raced down the steps.
At the bottom, I ran across the
room and leaped into the air.
This leap is called a *grand jeté*.
One day, my dad called me down to the basement.
He pointed up at the ceiling.

I looked and saw that part of the
ceiling was sagging.
It was the exact place where I landed
after each *grand jeté*!

The kids in my neighborhood
knew that I loved to dance.
I invited them to my house and gave ballet lessons
During the summer, we put on
shows in my friend Janie's garage.
Sometimes I even made my little brother, Danny,
dance with us.
We made the costumes out of old clothes.
My brother sold tickets to all the
parents in the neighborhood.
I had the biggest part in every show.
We always had a full audience.

ome adults thought it was funny

at I loved ballet so much.

ey laughed at me.

Iow sweet!" they said. "You want to be a ballerina."

Jo," I said to them, "I *will* be a ballerina."

When I was six years old,
Miss Willow closed her dance studio.
My mother quickly found a new ballet school.
This school was about fifteen minutes
away from our home.
My mom drove me there three times a week.
My new teacher's name was
Miss Bonnie McCullagh.
We put on many shows where we
danced and spoke our parts.
The Red Shoes and *Beauty and the
Beast* were two of my favorites.

t the end of the year, the students
the school put on a show for their parents.
was my first ballet recital.
[iss Bonnie picked me to do a dance all by myself.
chose to dance a scene from *Romeo and Juliet.*
danced the part where Juliet dies.
[y family, friends, and neighbors
l came to see me dance.
he adults who had laughed at me
eren't laughing now.
veryone who saw me dance that night
w that I was special.
oelieved I was special, too.

When I was eight years old,
I went on my first audition.
An audition is when you try out
for a part in a ballet.
My father drove me to the theater in Chicago.
The show I was trying out for was *The Nutcracker.*
I was very nervous!
I had always been the best in my class.
But now, I was being tested for the very first time.

I stood with a group of 150 children.
Many of the other children were
the best in their class, too.
A grown-up dancer showed us
different dance steps.

We had to repeat the steps while the dancer watched.
But I was so scared, I couldn't remember the steps.
I left without even trying.
I cried and cried.

About a week later, I got a letter from Miss Bonnie.
In the letter, she told me not to give up.
Even though I didn't get to be in the show,
it was good for me.
I learned an important lesson.
If I wanted to be a dancer, I could not give up.
I had to stand out at every audition.
I had to shine.

When I was ten years old, I needed braces.
But first I would have to have four teeth pulled.
That same summer, the New York City Ballet
came to Chicago.

COMING
SOON

THE
NEW YORK
CITY
BALLET

The dancers had come to perform
a ballet about a fairy kingdom.
The ballet was called *A Midsummer Night's Dream.*
Children were needed to dance the
parts of the butterflies and bugs.
I could hardly wait to try out.
But then I learned the bad news.
The tryout was on the very same day
as my dental appointment.

The dentist's office was a very busy one.
I had to go that day,
or I would have to wait many weeks.
That morning, my mother brought me
to the dentist.
He gave me medicine to make me sleep.
Then he pulled all four teeth
at once.

WHAT A CHARMING SMILE...

As soon as I woke up, I wanted to
try out for the ballet.
My mom was worried about me.
I was still very sleepy and in pain.
But I would not miss that audition.
Finally, my mother agreed and we were on our way.
When I arrived at the theater,
I saw hundreds of children.
All of the girls were wearing their hair up in buns.
But I thought I looked better with my hair down.

counted how many children were wearing glasses.

counted twenty-four.

decided to take mine off.

couldn't see very well.

Iy mouth really hurt.

was very nervous.

ut I remembered the *Nutcracker* audition.

promised myself that this time,

would get the part.

When the audition was over,
the director began to call out names.
One group of children was sent to the left.
The other group went to the right.
When my name was called, I was sent to the right.
Suddenly I got scared.
I was sure the children on the left
had gotten the parts.
So, I joined the group on the left.
Then I got a big surprise.

The group on the right had gotten the parts.
The group I had joined was being sent home!
I hurried over to the woman who auditioned us.
I explained the mix-up.
Luckily for me, she understood.
I got the part.

I had to learn the steps for
A Midsummer Night's Dream and
practice, practice, practice.
We practiced four hours every day for one week.
I was dancing the part of a bug.
I loved every minute.
But I didn't love my costume.
I wanted to be dressed like a fairy princess.
Instead, I had to wear green shorts and a helmet.
Still, I was never so happy.

On the night of the show, I waited backstage.
I felt dizzy and sick to my stomach.
What if I forgot the steps?
What if I fell?

Then there was no more time to worry.

I was onstage and I was dancing.

Somehow, when I started dancing,

I stopped being nervous.

I danced with true happiness.

Afterward, my family gave me flowers and hugs.

It was the night of my first

professional performance.

And it was perfect.

I got my first pair of toe shoes
when I was ten years old.
Toe shoes, or *pointe* shoes,
help a ballerina to stand on her toes.
Only one store in Chicago sold toe shoes.
My mother drove me there.

The woman at the store had me try on
many pairs.
Toe shoes must fit exactly,
or the dancer might hurt her feet.
We finally found the right pair.
As soon as I got home, I sewed on my ribbons.
Sewing ribbons on toe shoes is something
every ballerina learns.
I have worn many toe shoes,
but I will never forget my first pair.
I still have them!

When I was twelve, I began taking classes
at the Evanston School of Ballet.
It was forty-five minutes away from my home.
By this time, I was taking ballet classes
four or five times a week.

At the school, I practiced my
ballet steps for many hours.
I did each step hundreds of times,
trying to do them all perfectly.
My favorite step was the *arabesque*.
For this step, one leg is stretched out
behind the body.
The *arabesque* has always come easily to me
because I am flexible.
That means I am able to stretch
my arms and legs far.

But not all steps were easy for me.

The hardest thing for me to learn was the *pirouette*.

For this move, the dancer turns on one leg.

The other leg is either bent

or pointing out from the body.

Sometimes, I would lose my balance while turning.

This step is still very hard for me.

One day, I heard an announcement on the radio.
The Lyric Opera of Chicago was
holding auditions for ballet dancers.
All dancers had to be at least
sixteen years old to try out.
I went to the audition even though
I was only fourteen.
I danced for Maria Tallchief, a famous ballerina.
Miss Tallchief liked my dancing very much.
She let me join the ballet company.
Dancing with the Lyric Opera was hard work.
Miss Tallchief was very strict.
But I learned more about ballet
than I ever had before.

My greatest dream was to dance with
George Balanchine's ballet company,
the New York City Ballet.
I had never forgotten how wonderful it felt
to dance with that company in
A Midsummer Night's Dream.
George Balanchine was a very famous
choreographer, a person who makes ballets.
His school was the School of American Ballet.
It is very hard to get into the school
and even harder to get into the company.

At the age of sixteen, I was accepted
at the School of American Ballet.
Two years later, I became a member of
the New York City Ballet Company.
I was lucky to be able to dance for
George Balanchine.
Working with him was the greatest
experience I have ever had.
Mr. Balanchine was very kind.
Yet he made me work harder than
I ever thought possible.

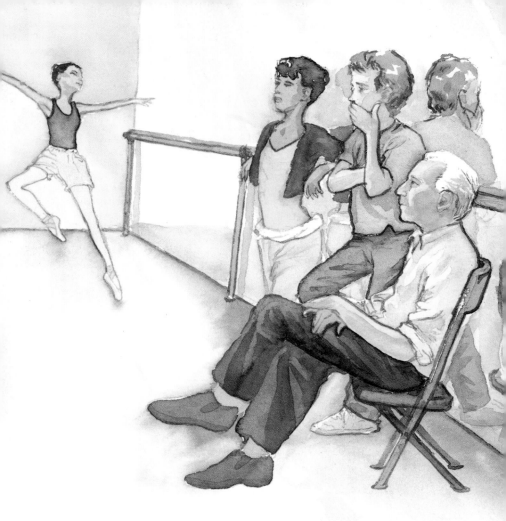

When I dance today, I can still
hear his voice in my head.
He used to say, "More! More!
What are you saving it for?"
Now, whenever I dance, I always try to give more.
Whether I am onstage or just practicing,
I always try my hardest.

Today I am a grown-up ballerina
with the New York City Ballet.
My day begins with a class at
ten-thirty in the morning.
Then, at noon, I practice for that night's show.
Rehearsal ends at six o'clock.
I try to eat some dinner and maybe take a nap.
At seven o'clock, I go to the theater.
I put on my stage makeup.

The makeup helps the audience to see my face.

It also hides the redness of my face.

When I dance, my face gets very red.

I wear my hair different ways for different parts.

Usually, my hair is in a bun.

At eight o'clock, the show begins.

By eleven o'clock, I am home.

Then I do it all again the next day!

Sometimes, I am very tired and my feet hurt.

I still get nervous before every show.

But I always love to dance on our

big stage at Lincoln Center in New York City.

We perform in other cities and
in foreign countries, too.
I have danced in Russia, England,
France, Japan, Denmark, and Taiwan.

A few years ago, I met a very handsome dancer
named Christian Claessens.
We got married and today we have
a beautiful little daughter named Joanna.

We opened a ballet school of our own.
My husband teaches there every day.
I teach on my days off from the ballet company.
Many of our students dream of
becoming ballet dancers.
I know that for some of them,
that dream will come true!

How to Sew Ribbons on Toe Shoes

Though each dancer does it differently, there are basic steps.

First, fold the heel down toward the inside of the shoe. The fold is where the ribbons should go.

Then, double the end of the ribbon and place it inside the shoe.

Sew the ribbon in place on each side of the shoe. Be sure to use extra-strong thread.

When wearing the shoes, the ribbons are tied next to the inside ankle bone. The ends should be tucked in.

How to Make a Ballerina Bun

To make a bun,
I put my hair in a
ponytail near the
top of my head.

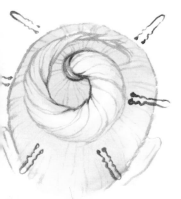

Then I twist the
hair around
and pin it in place.
I use lots of hair pins!

A hair net holds it
all in place.

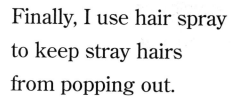

Finally, I use hair spray
to keep stray hairs
from popping out.

Some pretty flowers
or jewels pinned next to
the bun make me feel
especially beautiful.